The Wild Life of
OWLS

By Camilla de la Bédoyère

WINDMILL
BOOKS

THE WILD SIDE

Published in 2015 by **WINDMILL BOOKS,** an Imprint of Rosen Publishing
29 East 21st Street, New York, NY 10010

Publishing Director: Belinda Gallagher
Creative Director: Jo Cowan
Editorial Director: Rosie McGuire
Designers: Jo Cowan, Joe Jones
Image Manager: Liberty Newton
Production Manager: Elizabeth Collins
Reprographics: Stephan Davis, Anthony Cambray, Jennifer Cozens

ACKNOWLEDGEMENTS

The publishers would like to thank Mike Foster (Maltings Partnership), Joe Jones, and Richard Watson (Bright Agency)
for the illustrations they contributed to this book. All other artwork from the Miles Kelly Artwork Bank.

The publishers would like to thank the following sources for the use of their photographs: t = top, b = bottom,
l = left, r = right, c = center, bg = background, rt = repeated throughout. **Cover** (front) aksimilian/Shutterstock, (back)
Kaido Karner, (Speech panel) Tropinina Olga. **FLPA** 13(b) Adri Hoogendijk/Minden Pictures; 14(tr) Mike Jones; 19(b)
Erwin Van Laar/FN/ Minden. **Nature Picture Library** 7(tr) Dietmar Nill. **Photoshot** 7(bl) NHPA. **Shutterstock**
Joke panel (rt) Irzik; Heading panel (rt) PhotoDisc; Learn a Word panel (rt) Matthew Cole; 1 aksimilian; 3 Eric Isselée; 4–5
and 5(r) Eric Isselée; 6 Kaido Karner; 8(panel, t) LittleRambo; 9(b) BooHoo, wet nose, and Lyolya; 10 Ronnie Howard;
11(t) Daniel Hebert, (b) Rick Wylie; 12–13 alarifoto; 14(bl) and 15(m) Eric Isselée; 15(tr) Ronnie Howard; 16–17(bg)
Dementeva Marina&NatashaNaSt, 16(panel) yukipon, (r) Richard Laschon; 17(panel, tr) donatas1205, (tr) Dietmar Hoepfl,
(cl) Solid, (cr) LittleRambo; 18–19 Lori Labrecque; 21(tl) Eric Isselée, .(br) Stanislav Duben.

LIBRARY OF CONGRESS CATALOGING-IN-PUBLICATION DATA

De la Bédoyère, Camilla, author.
  The wild life of owls / Camilla de la Bedoyere.
      pages cm. — (The wild side)
  Includes index.
  ISBN 978-1-4777-5507-5 (pbk.)
  ISBN 978-1-4777-5506-8 (6 pack)
  ISBN 978-1-4777-5508-2 (library binding)
  1. Owls—Juvenile literature. I. Title.
  QL696.S8D45 2015
  598.9'7—dc23
                                   2014027102

Manufactured in the United States of America

CPSIA Compliance Information: Batch #CW15WM: For Further Information contact Rosen Publishing, New York, New York at 1-800-237-9932

Contents

I am an owl!

Owls are birds. We have feathers and we can fly. Our mouths are called beaks, or bills.

Hooked beak

Feathers

Q. How does a wet owl dry itself?
A. With a t-owel!

Wings

Two strong legs

4

Large eyes

Round face

Eurasian eagle owl
29.5 inches (75 cm) tall

Owl family
There are more than 200 species (types) of owl. The smallest could sit in your hand.

Sharp talons (claws)

Elf owl
5 inches (12.7 cm) tall

Great grey owl

Most owls eat small animals such as mice

I eat other creatures.

My sharp talons are perfect for catching them. Animals that hunt other animals are called predators.

Tasty bugs

Some owls swoop through the air to catch insects such as crickets and moths.

Scops owl

Fish dinner

Fishing owls use their strong talons to pluck fish and frogs from the water.

Fishing owl

Knock, knock.
Who's there?
Owl.
Owl who?
Owl be seeing you!

Activity time

Get ready to make and do!
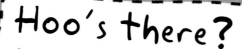

Hoo's there?
Owls have excellent hearing. How well do you and your friends hear? Take turns to close your eyes and listen to your friends as they each say "Twit-twoo." Can you figure out who is speaking?

Feathered friends

Ask for help!

YOU WILL NEED: pinecones · felt · leaves · scissors · double-sided tape · sticky tack

HERE'S HOW:
1. Cut felt shapes for the owl's eyes, beak and ear tufts, and tape them in place on the pinecone.
2. Tape a leaf "wing" to each side of the cone.
3. Add a small piece of sticky tack to the bottom of the cone to help your owl stand up.

Try making lots of different owls — use buttons, feathers, or shapes cut from card stock for the features.

Draw me!

YOU WILL NEED:
pencils · paper

Now color me in and give me a name!

1. Draw a big oval for the body and two circles for eyes.

2. Add small circles inside the eyes. Draw the beak and claws.

3. Draw a curved line on each side of the body for the wings, and add a branch.

Owl treats

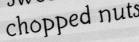

YOU WILL NEED:
· cupcakes or cookies
· white or chocolate icing
· a selection of cake decorations such as chocolate drops, silver balls, small sweets, dried fruit, chopped nuts

Ask for help!

HERE'S HOW:
Ice the tops of your cupcakes or cookies. Use the decorations to create owl faces on top.

Where do you live?

I live in trees.

From up here I can look down on the world below me. I even perch in a tree to sleep.

Great horned owl

LEARN A WORD:
perch
The way a bird stands on a branch with its toes wrapped around it.

10

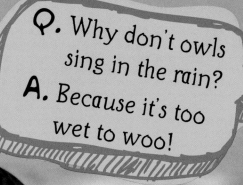

Q. Why don't owls sing in the rain?
A. Because it's too wet to woo!

Coldest owl

Snowy owls live near the North Pole where it is very cold. There are few trees, so the owls perch on the ground.

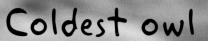

Snowy owl

Taking shelter

When it is rainy or windy, owls find a cozy hole in a tree or on the ground to sleep in. Some owls also shelter in caves and barns.

Little owl

How fast do you fly?

I fly more slowly than other hunting birds.

I spread my wings wide, and lean forwards. The wind catches my wings, and I soar through the sky.

Q. What do you call an owl with a low voice?

A. A growl!

Silent flight

Feathers soften the sound of an owl's wings. It can swoop down on a mouse before the mouse knows it is near.

Super sight

An owl's big eyes and good hearing help it to find mice moving in the grass, even when flying in the dark.

What are your babies called?

My babies are called chicks, or owlets.

Eggs and chicks

1 Chicks grow inside eggs. The eggs are almost round. They must be kept warm until they hatch.

2 The chicks have fluffy feathers to keep them warm in the nest.

Owlet

3 When it has grown its adult feathers the young owl is ready to fledge (fly away from the nest).

Fledgling

Find a nest

An owl doesn't build a nest for its eggs. It finds an old nest to lay its eggs in, or lays them in a hole in a tree.

Q. What do you call an angry owl?

A. A scowl!

Puzzle time

Can you solve all the puzzles?

Dinnertime

Ollie the owl has to catch two mice every day to feed his chicks. How many mice does he have to catch in three days?

ANSWER: Six

Wise owl

1. What type of animal is an owl – a bird or a bug?

2. Do snowy owls live in hot places or cold places?

3. What are an owl's claws called – toenails or talons?

ANSWERS: 1. A bird 2. Cold places 3. Talons

Tell us apart

There are three differences between Oscar and Otto – can you spot them?

Oscar

Otto

Which owl?

1. I eat bugs and my name rhymes with "pops."
2. I am the smallest owl and my name rhymes with "self."
3. I make a loud noise and my name rhymes with "peach."

Catch the mouse

Can you find a way through the maze to help Olive the owl catch the mouse?

What do you look like?

I am spotty and stripy.

Most owls have patterns on their feathers. They help us to hide in trees.

Screech owls

LEARN A WORD:
camouflage
Colors or patterns on an animal that help it to hide in its surroundings.

18

Q. What side of an owl has the most feathers?

A. The outside!

Hide-and-seek

Short-eared owls live in places with few trees. Their stripy feathers help camouflage them among plants on the ground.

What sound do you make?

Owls talk to each other.

Some sounds tell other owls to stay away. Others mean "I want to meet up." I am a barn owl and you may have heard my call.

"Twit-twoo"

Strange sound

I am a boobook owl and I am named after the noise I make!

"Boo-book"

Q. What do you call an owl with a sore throat?
A. A bird that doesn't give a hoot!

Not all owls hoot – some of them screech, hiss or whistle.

Spooky sound

I am a tawny owl and I hoot to tell other owls where I am.

"Ke-wick hoo hoo"

The Owl and the Pussycat

The Owl and the Pussycat went to sea
    In a beautiful pea-green boat,
They took some honey, and plenty of money,
    Wrapped up in a five-dollar note.
The Owl looked up to the stars above,
    And sang to a small guitar,
"Oh, lovely Pussy, oh, Pussy, my love,
    What a beautiful Pussy you are,
        You are,
        You are!
What a beautiful Pussy you are!"

Pussy said to the Owl, "You elegant fowl,
    How charmingly sweet you sing!
Oh, let us be married; too long we have tarried:
    But what shall we do for a ring?"
They sailed away for a year and a day,

To the land where the bong-tree grows;
And there in the wood a Piggy-wig stood,
  With a ring at the end of his nose,
    His nose,
    His nose,
With a ring at the end of his nose.

"Dear Pig, are you willing to sell for one shilling
  Your ring?" Said the Piggy, "I will."
So they took it away and were married next day
  By the Turkey who lives on the hill.
They dined on mince and slices of quince,
  Which they ate with a runcible spoon;
And hand in hand, on the edge of the sand,
  They danced by the light of the moon,
    The moon,
    The moon,
They danced by the light of the moon.

Edward Lear

23

Glossary

beak a bird's mouth

creature any kind of animal

fledge fly away from the nest

owlet a baby owl

pinecone the woody fruit of a pine tree

pluck take hold of something and quickly remove it from its place

quince a hard, pear-shaped fruit used in preserves or as flavoring

shelter a place where animals or people are kept safe

species a group of plants or animals that are all of the same kind

swoop move rapidly downward through the air

talons a bird's sharp claws

Index

barn 11, 20

beak 4, 8-9

camouflage 18-19

creature 6

feathers 4, 8, 13-15, 18-19

fledge 15

owlet 14

perch 10-11

pinecone 8

pluck 7

shelter 11

quince 23

snowy owl 11, 16

species 5

swoop 7, 13

talons 5-7, 16

Websites

For web resources related to the subject of this book, go to: **www.windmillbooks.com/weblinks** and select this book's title.

24